John Lash

Twins and the Double

with 153 illustrations, 16 in colour

Thames and Hudson

ART AND IMAGINATION

© 1993 Thames and Hudson Ltd, London

Printed and bound in Singapore by C.S. Graphics

Contents

Dyadic structure as illustrated in primitive and religious art often shows a remarkable grasp of mirror symmetry. Here the two figures joined at the feet are so mirror-similar that they can easily be misperceived as a single standing figure and its reflection. (Antipodal Figures. Guanacaste, Costa Rica.)

Twins and Twinning

In the realm of Twins the archetype of universal duality assumes a specific and spectacular form, manifesting its own set of unique and self-referential laws. Both as archetype and image, the matter of Twins appears at first clear and accessible, yet soon becomes elusive and baffling. Close examination reveals in a dramatic way the fluid and enigmatic nature of twinhood, insinuated by a cunning power that tempts the mind to fix it into tidy formulas, then teases the mind right out of them again.

Consider what happens each time we look into a mirror. There we behold our 'twin', the mirror-image of ourselves, seemingly a perfect likeness; yet this visual replica remains oddly, elusively different. The face in the mirror resembles our own in having identical features, but we hardly notice how these are criss-crossed, the left side of the actual face appearing on the right-hand side of the mirror-face and vice versa. In one stroke, the Twin reveals itself and tricks us, right before our eyes. We may go through our whole life without realizing that the face we see in the mirror is not the one that others see when they look directly at us.

To see how our face actually looks, we have to place two square mirrors together, at right angles to each other, and look directly at the seam. It takes *two* mirrors – a twin set of mirrors no less! – to restore the original image of the thing mirrored. In the Twin there resides a mercurial force that converts and deconverts whatever it encounters at will, according to its own laws. Each morning, standing before the mirror, we are already deeply implicated in its shifting realm of duplicity and substitution.

Certainly we are struck by the visual alikeness of human twins, but this impression is misleading and belies rather than exemplifies the innate structure of twinning. In a room of a hundred people it would not take long to pick out the identical twin sisters, but the remaining 98 people could be 49 sets of non-identical twins and you would not be able to detect them. In human reproduction twins exhibit these two variants, the identical and non-identical sets. Identical twins, born from the same ovum which has split in two, can be almost impossible to tell apart. Non-identical twins, born from separate ova, may bear no physical resemblance to each other. This two-case status applies for the archetype of Twins as well. In myth and legend, the most compelling examples of twinhood occur in the absence of physical resemblance.

In folklore and tribal customs surviving to this day (mostly in Africa), human twins are viewed as taboo regardless of whether or not they are identical look-alikes. Among the Yoruba and the natives of Dahomey, the birth of twins is greeted as an omen of good fortune, but among other tribes it is taken as the opposite, a curse so serious that the children are often killed and the mother permanently banished. All survivals of the twin-cult exhibit this radical ambiguity. The primitive mind intuits in twins the workings of an inscrutable power to be feared and revered, inspiring awe that goes quite beyond the novel impression made upon us by exact look-alikes.

Two-headed human births may have inspired ancient representations of two-headed dieties, but the archetype of duality transcends the rare case of biological twinning and points directly to the ambivalent nature of the Sacred. (Double-headed goddess from Gomolava.)

In Greco-Latin convention, Twins are most often associated with the astrological sign Gemini, referring to the heroes Castor and Pollux. Leda, their mother, wife of Tyndareus, was, while pregnant by her husband, visited by Zeus in the form of a swan, resulting in a double twin-birth, Castor and Pollux and Helen and Clytemnestra, of whom one of each pair was mortal (Castor and Clytemnestra, offspring of Tyndareus), the other immortal (Helen and Pollux, children of Zeus). This corresponds with the widespread folk belief that one twin is supernatural. Castor and Pollux, called the Dioscuri, have different temperaments but manage to agree and join in many heroic exploits together. This contrasts to the majority of mythical twin-sets where conflict and competition are prominent. Twins are a tight but troubled alliance.

A close parallel to the twin-motif appears in European folklore as the 'two brothers story', identified in some 770 variants.

Closely examined, Twins pose all manner of conundrums and inner contradictions. Ponder it as we will, the dynamic interfusion of Twins never lends itself to a clearcut exposition. Etymologically, 'twin' denotes both union and separation, joining and parting. In Middle English 'twin' was frequently used as a transitive verb: to twin something meant to split or divide it. An old adage says, 'We twa will never twin': we two will never be parted. But twin was also used to describe joining, juxtaposing or combining into one. Early on, both meanings seem to have been applied with equal emphasis, but later the word came more and more to denote coupling rather than separation.

'To twin' is a powerful action, and twinning permeates all of physical nature as well as all of our common and intimate activities of will, emotion and thinking. Doubling, or replication, is the active mode of duality, but this is not to be mistaken for the harmonious balancing-act of pure opposites. As the mirror tells, Twins are not to be taken for identical pairs. Rather than a model of perfect symmetry, they embody the trick proposition of errant near-symmetry. A photograph of the mirror-face will not overlay the actual face, for twins are not superimposable units, nor pure opposites, nor complementaries. They do not fit the neat category of duality that encompasses harmonic polarities such as *Yin* and *Yang*, dual components of the *Tao* in Chinese metaphysics.

By a broad-based definition, Twins are the special case of duality in its mode of self-contradiction, the *non-resolving duad*. Since they are not 'polar opposites,' they will not resolve into a final and harmonic unity. Twins are parity and disparity, but equality – never.

As disparity, twinhood is rampant in our world, in ways far more widely evident than the ideal model of harmonic opposites interlocked in perfect union, neat as two peas in a pod. Our hands, for instance, are a set of twins exhibiting attributes of likeness and disparity *simultaneously*. They match when we place them palm to palm in the gesture of prayer, but mismatch when we try to fit one into the glove that belongs to the other, or when we try to manage a tool or switch with the 'wrong hand.' (In keeping with the shiftiness of Twins, the wrong hand can be either hand.) In the obvious 'twinning' of our hands, the way they match is not more significant than the way they don't. Throughout countless variations, Twins play off similarity and difference against each other in ways that never fail to baffle and fascinate. A 'matching set' of anything (bookends, for instance) is a rare, innocent case of twinning. In many more cases, Twins are a duo who look as if they should coincide and complement each other, but never actually do. Or, never *quite* do.

The phenomenon of near-coincidence, fusing similarity and difference, pervades the natural world in that peculiar feature defined by the awkward term 'handedness.' Things like crystals, seashells, galaxies, water spiralling down a drain, animal horns, twining vines and curly hair possess either right- or left-handedness. Here Twins are revealed in the odd feature of *parity*, a mark of nature's ways that seems to imply a profound but elusive lawfulness. The human umbilical cord, for instance, occurs exclusively in a left-handed spiral — but why? The great French doctor, Louis Pasteur, was convinced that parity, if it could be systematically understood (which it can't), would reveal to us the deepest secrets of universal formation.

We are fascinated by twins without knowing exactly what it is that fascinates us, but such is the nature of twinning. Twins lure and elude. Consider, for example, the optical illusion of facing profiles, black on a white background, which become the outlines of a chalice, white on a black background. Here is twinning twice-over: the profiles face to face are twins to each other, and the facing profiles, taken as a set, are twin to the chalice. In other words, as profile is twin to profile, the profiles together are twin to chalice. In the first case the twinning appears as an obvious visual duplication, in the second case, as an elusive but equally vivid visual conversion, shifting profiles into chalice and chalice back again into profiles.

In some way which eludes rational comprehension, twinning demonstrates an odd *generative* power. Gazing at the optical illusion, we can see the specific components of it with no difficulty, but there is something else as well, something we cannot quite see, which behaves with a perverse autonomy before our eyes.

Among the alchemists this shifty, ambivalent behaviour was said to be encountered at intimate moments of mastering the Art. It indicated the presence of a fluidic entity they called *Mercurius Duplex*, believed to be the crucial agent in the 'Great Work' of transforming nature.

Taken more intimately, then, the Twin proves to be something more than the product of straightforward duplication. It cannot be confined to the simple case of visual look-alikes, or the literal instance of two creatures born almost at the same time from a single womb. Naturally these cases catch our attention, but the true power of the Twin lures us toward a deeper and more troubling set of perceptions. Biological twins, in fact, prove to be merely a special and limited case of the larger category of the archetype, which includes the Double and other variants, such as the rivals, scapegoat and soul-mate.

Far more complex then it first appears, the matter of Twins requires us to develop a sophisticated version of 'duality theory'. One early and well-framed contribution to this task comes down to us from the Greek philosopher, Empedocles (c490–430 BC), who proposed that the elemental quaternary – the composition of the four Elements (Earth, Air, Fire, Water), which comprises all things in creation including the human form and psyche – is itself informed by the counterplay of two master principles, Eros and Strife. The first he described as the power of organic unity and mutual attraction, the second as the power of disparity and random disruption. In all things, Eros and Strife (or Desire and Division) are continually interacting, aligning themselves and then displacing each other. Dual generative powers of creation, they are incapable of existing independently.

In the language of William Blake, these are 'warring contraries' that perpetually invade and repel each other. 'Without contraries there is no progression,' wrote Blake in *The Marriage of Heaven and Hell*. And likewise, there is no desire without division.

We have noted the contrast between identical and non-identical sets of twins in human births and how the same distinction applies for the archetype. As we shall see, throughout its many variants in world mythology, cultic and religious activity, art and literature, the factor of exact resemblance is rarely emphatic. The story of Jacob and Esau in the Old Testament (Genesis 3) illustrates a number of the laws stated above, presenting us with a much more complex set of interactions than would occur if the two brothers were exact look-alikes. In fact, it is the dissimilarity of the twin brothers that counts in the story, which tells us that Esau is 'red and hairy' while Jacob is 'smooth.' Already in the womb they are enmeshed in conflict – a widespread motif, found also in the myth of Isis and Osiris and South American twin-lore. Esau is the elder, born first, and then Jacob follows 'with his hand grasping Esau's heel', an image of subservience and competition. When the time comes for the elder son to receive the blessing of his father, Jacob contrives to receive it in his place. By the right of primogeniture, the fate of the twins is distinguished, but Jacob wants what Esau is due: motif of desire-and-division. To get it, Jacob covers his arms with a fleece to impersonate his brother's coarse-natured hairiness. The aged father, nearly blind at eighty, readily mistakes the younger son for the elder and confers his blessing. Several themes converge here: rivalry, substitution, imitation, transference (of the birthright).

Elsewhere in mythology and folklore, Twins are strongly charged with taboo, valencies of interdiction and persuasion. Their baffling power lies in their ambiguity and the generative force of their off-balance bonding, taken by the primitive mentality as a sure mark of the Sacred. In fact, nowhere is sacred ambivalence more deeply and vividly embodied than in the archetype of Twins. This ambivalence of spiritual power is what allows it to operate, alternately, as a wounding and a healing influence, as that which generates order or disorder as if by caprice. While the modern, rational mind wants to resolve this terrible inconsistency of the Sacred in a final closure or all-encompassing aim, both ancient and aboriginal peoples prefer to accept it as it is, without looking for a way to bargain ourselves out of the dilemma.

Our best chance to understand Twins is, perhaps, to designate them uniquely as an 'ambitype' so that we are always reminded of the frequent and unpredictable change-of-rules operating within this special and seminal case of archetypal patterning. Then it will be clear that all twins are indeed counterparts, but not all counterparts are twins. A couple of apples is not a set of twin apples. Twins are *idiosyncratic* pairs, a duo precariously bonded by certain activities and principles, such as inversion, substitution and the others stated above. Poison one of the two apples and substitute it for the other, and they will become twins. Make the first, unpoisoned apple the cure for the fatal poison of the other, and you have the plot-line for a quest tale based on twin-motifs. Likewise, if one apple is reflected in a mirror, it becomes the twin of its counterpart, or if one apple is reflected in two separate mirrors, the mirror-apples are twins of each other as well as twins of the original. This reveals yet again the odd, astonishing exponential vigour in twinning, the facile elaboration of 2^n, duality carried to the nth power.

'Twin' derives from a common set of roots such as TWI-, ZWI-, TVI, the Latin BI- and the Greek DI-, all related through the Indo-European base DVI- or DVA-, 'two, duality'. The same root occurs in 'twine' and 'twilight'. Twine is twisted thread, like DNA, the master chemical directing all processes of life and death, and twilight is the dual and ambiguous state where dark and light intermingle. In a lucid intuition of twinning, Goethe proposed a theory of colour that rejects the Newtonian breakdown of 'white light' into the sevenfold spectrum. Instead, he described light commingling with darkness to produce all variations of colour as a series of colloidal, or plasma-like, states. Here light and darkness figure as the ultimate set of twins, according with a great many mythologies around the world. They appear as Horus and Set, the embattled twins, as the twin-gods, Balder and Hodur, in Scandinavian myth, and so forth. They are the embryonic primaries whose perpetual, off-balance interplay informs all events in creation at the same time as it evades all attempts to define it in terms of fixed positions or clear-cut polarities.

Twin Gods and Firstborn Parents

With Twins it is tempting to suppose a solid foundation for all the contrary and ambivalent patterns they exhibit, but in the final analysis twinhood does not appear to rest on a monistic basis. This is proven by the high incidence of twin deities and firstborn pairs in cosmogonic mythologies, worldwide. The primacy of *dyadic structure* is clear, for instance, in Central American mythology, where the very oldest of the gods is designated by the prefix *OME-*, meaning 'two': hence the names of the primordial ancestors: Ometecuhtli and Omecihuatl, 'two-chief' and 'two-woman'.

Sometimes it is the creator-gods, and sometimes it is the first generation of created beings (proto-human), who appear as twins, and then again, sometimes the types are mixed. In the *Kojiki*, the Japanese creation-myth, the cosmogonic deities, Izanagi and Izanami, are also a typical brother/sister pair, like Isis and Osiris in Egyptian myth. They stand upon the rainbow bridge over the chaos of the uncreated cosmos and thrust the 'Jewel Spear of heaven' down into the formless womb of the waters below. An island coagulates at the tip of the spear – *ono-koro*, 'self-churning' – and there they descend to their island home to become the parents of all races. Their union is ritualized by a ceremonial walk around a central pillar, *axis mundi*, or what is called the 'axis of twinning' in the structure of interlocking crystals.

Here, as may so often happen, the language of myth approximates to the language of science: 'island-universe' being the exact term in astrophysics for our galaxy, the rotating structure of regular spiral arms generated by the twin-gods of gravity and centrifugal motion. Its form, seen from above, is a clockwise or 'right-hand' spiral, a pure enantiomorph which is not superposable on its mirror-image. All this is aptly described by the ritual dance of the ancestral Pair. The power of twinning is present at the dawn of creation.

In cases where the cosmogonic deities are clearly distinguished from the firstborn Pair, the former are sometimes not represented as twins, but this belies a later, monistically biased construction, overlaid on the prelogical intuition of dyadic structure. Whenever 'First Principles' fall into generation, twins appear prolifically. They are the omnipresent culture-heroes and ancestral heads of the great clans, races and civilizations.

In the Judaeo-Christian creation-myth, a single and supreme being, Yaweh, produces a primordial pair – a good example of the monistic hypothesis subsuming the dyad. Adam and Eve are not explicitly cited as twins, but criteria for twinning are present in their interactions. Adapted to reflect a monistic (i.e., masculine) bias, Eve emerges, rather insignificantly and after the fact, from Adam's side. From the outset, these firstborn parents are enmeshed in a conflict defined by the interplay of desire and division, as well as other twin-motifs. In a typical dyadic action of luring and antagonizing, Eve is said to tempt Adam with the apple used by the Serpent to tempt her: motif of mimetic desire, Adam comes to want what Eve wanted after the Serpent showed her what was to be wanted. Satan has prevailed against God (competition), the clear division between mortal and immortal is corrupted (substitution of values), and the First Pair are cast out of Eden (transference).

One important variant of the myth includes another woman, Lilith, who figures as the demonic half-sister or twin-sister of Adam. As Adam's 'first wife', Lilith is a female double of the First Man, created from dust as his twin and equal. In Sumerian *lil* means 'wind', while Adam refers to the inert element of earth or material substance. This parallels exactly the dyadic cosmogonies of the East (Shiva/Shakti, Purusha/Prakriti, and so on) in which the male aspect of creation is held to be inert and passive (the onlooker) while the female is dynamic, like the wind. Clearly, Adam–Lilith is the more archaic twin-set of First Parents, but Lilith is rejected and, as we read in Isaiah 34:14, cast out into the realm of wild dogs, screech owls and satyrs. In many creation-myths a similar loss or slurring of decisive twin-motifs is probable, due to late adaptations and corrupt recensions. Generally the rule is, the more primitive, the more dyadic.

To a very great extent, Egyptian theology reveals a late, rigorous systemization of mythological material which retains the intricacies of archaic dyadic structure. In the creation-myth preserved at Heliopolis the cosmogonic deities are the twins, Atun and Nun, comparable to sperm and ovum. Nun is chaos – passive, all-receiving, all-congealing – the image of Desire which attracts and holds. Atun is epigenetic, an entity capable of self-articulation and separation – in the same way a single sperm separates itself from the wriggling horde of 300 million others: i.e., by individuation, or Division. These two produce the first-born offspring of the world-creating gods, Ra, who then replicates himself in twin forms, Khepera, the Beetle, and Bennu, the Phoenix, clear images of materialization and regeneration. Via these twin powers, the mothering and fathering potencies imparted to him through his parents, Ra then initiates the scenario of world-creation, but he does not produce any animate beings to inhabit it – a clear (and rare) distinction between cosmogenesis and anthropogenesis. Creature-making proceeds again from the twin deities, Atun and Nun, through their replication in another set of twins offspring, Shu and Tefnut. Shu, whose name derives from a root indicating 'to raise', performs this epic feat of Division and separates heaven by raising it above the earth. For her part, Tefnut generates order and cohesion, in keeping with her role as an avatar of the mothering powers of Eros, primordial Desire.

These two also consort to produce yet another set of twins, Geb and Nut, Earth and Sky, who are animate beings as well as cosmic environments. Geb and Nut in turn produce quadruplets, Isis/Osiris and Nephthys/Set. In Plutarch's elaborate account, Isis and Osiris conjoin in the womb of Nut to produce the seed of their son, Horus, even before they are born. This introduces the complex motif of 'royal incest' which appears frequently in twin lore. Uterine incest is a sacred motif related to the obscure interbreeding rites of the Pharaonic families, believed to have been controlled by the priesthood for the purpose of producing genetic freaks or hybrids who were then viewed as specific embodiments of superhuman deities. In the system of theocratic lineage, the ongoing generations of god-kings were maintained by these genetic mutations who were held to be successive avatars of a single assumed deity: Sesostris I-III, Thutmosis I-IV, Ramses I-XI (a particularly hardy strain) and so on. The Pharaohs

In Egyptian myth, the ram-headed God Khnum, spinning the potter's wheel, creates the human being and its double simultaneously. Every being is created dual, i.e., from the matrix of dyadic structure. (Khnum creating human and double.)

While doubles may be attributed to all things, the power to project the double is considered as an act of magical force, possessed only by the gods and their human counterparts, the sorcerers and shamans. Projection of the double is mimetically illustrated in masks and fetish-figures. (Africa, Bobo mask.)

were designer twins, even designated by two titles, one for the body (*chm*) and one for the avatar using it (*nishwt*).

Although, unfortunately, it can inspire the wildest speculations, such as scenarios of extraterrestrially managed 'genetic engineering', the practice of royal incest in Egypt and elsewhere is an incontestable fact, lending serious weight to the notion that primitive and prelogical societies possessed a working knowledge of genetic structure, *which they always represented in dyadic terms.*

As Mircea Eliade has demonstrated in his comparative studies, the *coincidentia oppositorum* is the most favoured way to describe the paradox of creation in all mythologies. The intuition of dyadic generation is deeply rooted in the human mind, going back to prehistory, even though the mechanics of it have only become scientifically defined since the discovery of the structure of DNA in 1953. Invariably, the Cosmic Giant or Primordial God is dual and androgyne, as seen in the Hindu icon of Shiva-Kali, the Ardhanarishvara, a twin-entity, male on one side, female on the other. No doubt this religious image did not emerge without reference, somewhere down the line, to the actual appearance of Siamese twins, an awesome feat of nature. Although the Ardhanarishvara is not two-headed (probably because it represents an idealized version of twinning, with the dyadic features reduced as far as possible to a unity), there occur in Western alchemical manuscripts many versions of the Divine Androgyne which could as well be close anatomical renderings of actual Siamese twins.

Visual lore on the Divine Twins is rich enough, and oral lore even more so. Among the pre-Incan culture of Peru, the creator-god was called Atachuchu, 'Lord of the Twins'. He produced the first man as a magical projection of his own double, a favourite device of twinning in shamanic cultures. This human double then mates with a woman of a dark or shadowy race, like the sinister Lilith or the daughters found by Cain in the East of Eden. Becoming pregnant, she produces a set of twin eggs (image of dizygotic reproduction, the more common instance of two-egg fertilization which results in 'fraternal' or non-identical twins) and dies giving birth, as must have frequently happened in primitive times when singleton birth was already enormously dangerous for the mother.

From the eggs emerge the twin brothers, Apocatequil and Piguerao, the former being first-born and the more powerful. Apocatequil touches his mother's corpse and revives her to life, then he slays the race of dark people who had maliciously destroyed the father-god right after the conception of the twins, and goes on to perform all manner of benevolent deeds leading to the formation of the pre-Incan peoples and their culture. Of his lesser brother, little is known, but this is typical of oral twin lore which, most often, does not reflect a fair and equitable treatment of the twins.

The Pre-Incan twins are, like Castor and Pollux, attributed with rain-making powers, control over thunderbolts, fertilization, protection of travellers, and so forth. Firstborn twins are generally remembered as benevolent to the race or culture they have served, but they may also be represented as adversaries who battle over its fate. At the base-level of psychic potency, they embody the tension of deep, irresolvable conflicts registered in the ancestral memory of our race by violence which has saved the day at one moment and ruined it all the next.

This may account, in part at least, for the stark terror that surrounds the birth of twins in aboriginal and archaic societies. Folklore and practices surviving to this day abound with chilling examples of how humankind has attempted to constrain the torsion and torment of the conflictual forces twins embody. In

Africa, in the Niger Delta, both twins are immediately slain and their mother cast out of the community. The taboo is so severe that the twins cannot even be buried and must be executed in a ritual manner: a slave woman breaks their backs on her knee and they are cast into the underbush. In Nigeria, it is a curse to say, 'May you become the mother of twins,' and the making a V-sign with the fingers (as politicians since Churchill have done to signal confidence or 'Victory') is a gesture of damning. Among the Arebo, a man unfortunate enough to have a wife who bears twins may redeem her life by paying for an alternative victim: motif of substitution, closely associated to scapegoating (as described later).

All across Africa the twin-cult is strong, and in some areas there are even 'twin-towns' where the outcast mothers and their offspring live. In some cases, one twin is kept and the other is killed, usually by live burial. Among the Bantu of the Lower Congo, one twin is starved and buried at a crossroads, traditional burial site for scapegoats and those struck by lightning, while the other twin is given a cross-image of his counterpart to maintain their supernatural link.

In the Amazon, twins are considered to be subnatural, if not completely subhuman. The same holds true among many tribes in North America, who kill both twins, and among the Aborigines of Australia, where twins are viewed as agents of evil, presenting a grave danger to the harmony of the community. Nevertheless, in Australian lore twins figure strongly among the totemic ancestors, such as the two sisters in the Djanggwul song-cycles and the two Dreamtime wanderers, the Mamandabari. Usually, they are close allies, but not always. In the Kimberly district, however, the Dreamtime ancestors (*wondjina*) known as the Lightning Brothers, Wagtjabbulla and Tcubuinji, quarrel over the wife of the elder one, leading to serious disorders in the land. But whether the mythical twins quarrel or not in ancestral tales, the taboo applies to their biological counterparts across the board, as it were. Twins are dangerous either way: because they incarnate the forces of supernatural conflict, or because they reproduce the image of cosmic near-symmetry in a literal manner which violates the boundaries of the secret, invisible realm where those forces are believed to originate.

These alarming customs stand in contrast to others which are, unfortunately, far less prevalent. For the Togo of West Africa, and for the Masai, twins are fetish-children, too powerful to kill, whose taboo must be adapted to the well-being of the community. Wherever twins are honoured and revered, at least one of them is always treated as the progeny of a totemic ancestor or power-animal. For the Togo, twins are doubles of the long-tailed monkey, or even of Ohoho, their supreme deity, and the last-born is considered of higher rank. In Sakhalin, off the east coast of Siberia, twins are viewed as the offspring of a normal father and a wizard so wily he conceals which one is his, so each must be treated with the extreme care accorded to taboo.

In twinhood, always, we encounter the fundamental ambivalence of the sacred according to which the same power can both reveal and conceal, cure and wound. Although modern, logic-based thinking, stemming from the Greeks, makes every possible attempt to surmount this ambivalence, the mythic imagination embraces it. Also, the primitive mentality is, by necessity, extremely pragmatic, as far as it goes. Where the errancies and inequities of nature and human affairs are painfully evident, twin-motifs fit more often than not. Since these cruel irregularities cannot be controlled, all manifestations of twinning are carefully honoured.

Like the Dreamtime ancestors of Australia, the totemic ancestor-gods of the Egyptians are entities who incorporate the power of animal doubles and therefore are often shown as theriomorphic in face and figure. (Sekhmet, Egyptian statue.)

The Bond of Rival Brothers

Not only is rivalry a key theme in the dynamics of Twins, as we have already noted, but it is in some cases the primary mark designating two entities as Twins, even if they do not meet the strict definition of near simultaneous birth from the same womb.

Curiously, the rivalry of mythological twins is not reflected in what we know about the relationship between human twins. On the contrary, twins for the most part are easy and amicable with each other, if not deeply dependent. They exhibit emotional complicity, telepathic rapport and, in general, a playful sense of getting along as only twins can do. If either or both of them become pathological, however, their behaviour between themselves and toward others will assume uncanny parallels to mythological patterns of imitation and rivalry.

The bonding of rival twins is illustrated over and over again in trickster tales of the Americas, where one twin is strong and wily, the other weak and dull-witted, yet always capable of enough ingenuity to confound the activities of his superior. In the Iroquoian folk-cycles, for instance, the first being is a woman named Ataensic who falls from the sky and lands on a turtle's back, where she gives birth to an unnamed daughter. The girl becomes mysteriously pregnant and bears twins, Tawiscara and Iosheka. The first is so unruly and malicious that he is unwilling to wait to be born in a natural manner. He breaks out of his mother's side, killing her as he does so. Iosheka, the good twin, goes about the earth serving the needs of nature, providing water and so forth, but Tawiscara interferes in his good efforts — for instance, producing a monstrous frog to swallow up all the water. Eventually, Iosheka vanquishes his evil brother and performs the many benevolent deeds typical of the culture-hero.

Very similar motifs occur in the conflict between Romulus and Remus, associated with the foundation of Rome. Among the kings of Alba Longa, in the pre-Roman era, there arose a factional dispute between two brothers, the younger of whom seized the throne. He placed his daughter, Rhea Silvia, in the sanctuary of the Vestal Virgins, but she was raped by the god Ares and gave birth to twins, Romulus and Remus. The king ordered the boys to be drowned, but they were found and suckled by a she-wolf, then adopted by a peasant. When he founded Rome, Romulus ploughed a furrow to mark the line for the city wall and when Remus jumped over it, his brother slew him. Here Remus represents the threat of divisive violence (disagreement over boundaries) and Romulus represents the authority to constrain it.

In the conflict between Twins, the fate of one may be decided by the superior strength of the other, or by a seemingly accidental factor or event. This illustrates the arbitrary and haphazard nature of violence, making it a matter of great awe to the primitive mind. In some cases there is no apparent conflict at all, and one twin will appear as inferior from the outset, having no chance to overmaster the other. This illustrates the ruthless inequity of nature, the way the balance of forces is continually shifting. Yet the presence of the lesser, weaker twin often highlights the superiority of the other, and in little clues here and there we discover how the power of the lesser twin does come into play against the greater one.

The Grecian myth of Herakles and Iphikles is a clear instance of this point. Heracles is born first, on the second day of the (new) moon, and Iphikles, the weaker twin, on the fourth day. Apart from this we hear almost nothing about the character and deeds of Iphikles, but the lesser twin in this tale does not disappear completely. Some sources say he departs from home and parents to enter the service of a Peloponnesian chieftain, Eurystheus, lord of Mycenae. It happens to be this very same Eurystheus who assigns to Heracles the Twelve Labours for which he gains his fame. From the background, as it were, the lesser twin exerts a conflictual challenge against his brother. Heracles appears to compensate for this by taking along Iolaos, the son of Iphikles, as his companion in the labours. As with so many twin tales, the fine decisive details of the conflict are largely lost or obscured.

In twin lore the only consistencies are found in the parallel structure, or isomorphism, of the motifs. The well-known case of Esau and Jacob includes struggle in the womb, a motif paralleled in Iroquois legend (previously described) as well as in Persian myth where Ahriman, the evil-doing spirit, breaks prematurely out of the womb. Isomorphism applies again between the Jacob–Esau conflict and the struggle between their ancestors, Cain and Abel. Abel is also the younger, the second son of Adam. The slaying of Abel by Cain is repeated, with expanded detail, in the drama of Esau and Jacob, showing how the twin-motif can encompass a long-term karmic pattern running down through the generations. In the drama of Christ, where the primordial karma of humankind can be said to consummated, twin-motifs appear in staggering profusion (as described below).

Mimesis, or imitation, has been celebrated in Western tradition for its educative and culture-generating effects, but it has also a conflictual aspect of considerable impact. How complexly nuanced the problem was for our ancestors is dramatically conveyed in a tale of rival twins preserved on papyrus from the time of Ramses II, around 1250 BC. The tale of *Anpu and Bata* was, specifically, the ancestral inspiration for the Horus–Set conflict that dominates Egyptian religion and, generally, the precedent of almost every other twin-struggle one can name.

The tale is very complex, with no fewer than twenty interworking motifs, but some common conflictual factors are immediately evident. Bata is the gentle one of the pair, who tends his brothers cattle and understands their language. He is warned by the animals that Anpu's wife will attempt to seduce him, so he flees, but Anpu chases him and finally Bata wounds himself, as if he had committed a crime, when in fact he is totally innocent. Bata assumes the role of scapegoat, the innocent victim who will expiate the sin committed by another — or in this case, the very idea of sin in the mind of Anpu's wife. The gods then create a wife-double for Bata, who is in turn lusted after by the Pharaoh, in the same way that Anpu's wife lusted after Bata. When the wife tells the Pharaoh the secret of Bata's totemic identity (twinning) with the acacia tree, the Pharaoh cuts down the tree and Bata dies. Anpu, now realigned with his brother by an odd switch of the type so frequent in twin tales, looks for Bata and revives him in the form of a bull, but the bull, brought before the Pharaoh, is killed at Bata's wife's request! This is double jeopardy, Egyptian-style: Bata dies twice, his death itself is twinned. When his blood springs up overnight into Persea trees, the wife orders them to be cut down and a chip flies into her mouth, impregnating her, so that Bata is again reborn, a third time, now the son of his own wife-twin.

Finally, when the old Pharaoh dies, Bata becomes lord of the land and on his authority has his wife killed. When he dies, Anpu inherits the kingdom. The tale ends on a reconciliatory note, although this is still a long way from the equivalent of peacemaking between the brothers.

Rivalries of an equally complex kind are rampant in the surviving lore of the

Opposite: The dominant figure in Mexican mythology is the twin-god Quetzalcoatl, Lord of the Morning Star (the emblem of which is shown here in a beautiful detail at the centre of the stela), who wages a constant battle with his dark counterpart, Tezcatlipoca, Lord of the Smoking Mirror. Their parallels in Persian myth are Orhmazd and Ahriman. (Stela. Quetzalcoatl.)

Indian tribes of the Americas, both North and South. By far the most widespread category of rival twins in Amerindian lore consists of one benevolent spirit and one trickster or evil-doer who continually spoils, or attempts to spoil, the good efforts of the other. The nature of these fraternal rivalries is magically fluid, of course. Love and Strife are interchangeable, and brothers who assist each other one moment may be at odds the next. In the lodges and kivas the tales of trickster-twins are told with a mixture of solemnity and hilarity.

Amerindian twin rivalry is closely comparable with Persian dualism, the most archaic category of twin-strife in written evidence. In this ancient theology, Ohrmazd and Ahriman are deities represented as 'twin sons' of Zurvan, the supreme being. Ohrmazd is the offspring produced by a generous act of sacrifice on the part of Zurvan, who hopes thereby to work up something good out of the pre-cosmogonic void, but Ahriman comes forth as the expression of the creator-god's doubt about the final consequences of the good intentions. Here, in a line, is a profound cosmological premise, fraught with theological and moral issues which are still relevant.

In the womb of Zurvan – that is, in the primeval void before creation – the twins are not comfortable with each other, and Ahriman breaks out first, exhibiting a ferocious prematurity and aggressiveness, such as we often find in the earlier and stronger twin. Although he should be the second-born – because doubt, you must agree, follows intention – he assumes the rights of the first-born (motif of substitution) and demands to rule over the dawning creation. Zurvan, in his galactic avataric form of Akarana Zurvana, introduces linear time as a solution to this demand: he assigns to Ahriman the rulership over creation for a limited period, after which Ohrmazd will prevail for ever. This motif is duplicated in Christian eschatology of Christ overcoming for eternity the thousand-year rule of Satan – a direct borrowing, in fact.

We see that Iranian dualism, even in most archaic form, is ontologically sophisticated and profoundly based in dyadic structure. The bond of Ohrmazd and Ahriman divides the world and unites all its inhabitants. Eros and Strife thrive under the sign of the Twins.

Doubles, or Metamorphic Twinning

The Double belongs unquestionably to the dark side of world mythology and folklore. It represents duality in its most perplexing and sinister aspect: the Twin as monstrous or metamorphic duplicate of its original. In the annals of anthropological fieldwork, it assumes an enormous range, there being hundreds of specific terms for the double in folklore from Australia to Finland, Mexico to Melanesia. Even more potent than straightforward twinning, doubling *involves the risk that the duplicate will overwhelm and consume the powers of the entity which generates it.*

Nothing is more common to primitive mentality than the idea of doubling a person or thing by way of an image or object, even a name. The cliché says the 'savage' does not let his picture be taken for fear that his soul will thereby be stolen – but it is not quite so simple as that. The soul can be duplicated in an image, but the mere act of duplicating does not threaten to divest the native of his soul. The image itself is the problem. It can serve as a potential reservoir, a medium capable of drawing vital and spiritual force from its original, or transmitting impressions to it from afar. What is done to the image is done to the owner.

Here, of course, is the basis of voodoo spells, 'sympathetic magic' as described by Frazer, and all manner of occult rites and practices which exploit the twin-dynamics of imitation, substitution and transference.

A primary danger posed by doubles is well illustrated in the Greco-Latin myth of Narcissus, a beautiful youth captivated by his own reflection. In the story the twin-motif also appears in the figure of Echo, the nymph who repeats what the gods have said so that other gods can hear it. When Narcissus rejects her due to his self-absorption (motif of desire-and-division), she calls down a curse upon him. He then becomes so enamoured of his own image that he wastes away. Solipsistic deviance and subversion of Eros are typical of the double, an entity which possesses enormous devitalizing powers.

In itself, mirror-reflection effects a close shift between the *image* in its passive, purely reflexive status and the *entity* which comes potently and autonomously alive in the Double. The looking-glass is a zone of dangerous transition, rightfully surrounded by awe and taboo for the primitive mentality. Mirrors provide the readiest direct form of magical duplication. Not surprisingly, they figure strongly in a number of twin-based creation-myths, worldwide. In Japan, the Sun-goddess, Amaterasu, retreats into a cave after the world is devastated by the unruly storm-god, Susano. All of nature suffers from the lack of sunlight until Amaterasu is lured out again by glimmers emanating from her own reflection in a mirror, held up just outside the mouth of the cave.

A parallel, far more complex mirror-motif plays decisively in the struggle between the twin-gods, Quetzalcoatl and Tezcatlipoca, in Mexican mythology from Toltec sources. The virgin sky-mother, goddess of the writhing serpent-petticoat, Coatlicue, swallows a feather and gives birth to twins, who become perpetual enemies. Quetzalcoatl is the culture-hero and benevolent teacher of humankind, while Tezcatlipoca (or Huitzilopochtli, his Aztec variant) is an evil sorcerer and necromancer, a prototype of the 'Black Magician' at his best (or worst). Quetzalcoatl resists the temptation to acquire power through performing human sacrifices, because he loves and reveres the noble human form, which he believes himself to resemble; but when Tezcatlipoca, Lord of the Smoking Mirror, shows him his own reflection in the black obsidian looking-glass, he is shocked to see how haggard and non-human he looks. Next Tezcatlipoca persuades him to alter his appearance by adorning himself in cosmetics and finery, so that he resembles a beautiful young boy, and then tempts him further to violate taboo by drunkenness and incestuous sex. When he recovers, Quetzalcoatl is so ashamed that he flees into exile but with a promise to return, to resurrect himself and appear at a later time.

The 'smoking mirror' of Tezcatlipoca is an occult tool of duplication which allows the black magician to take control of whoever looks into it. The Nahua word *tezcat* means 'obsidian', the same hard, black, mirror-like stone used to make the sacrificial blades for cutting out the heart of the victims chosen for human sacrifice, in huge numbers, in the horror show of Aztec religious ceremony. In these elaborate rites, a young man was chosen to imitate the series of temptations which defeated Quetzalcoatl. For a year he was magnificently adorned, allowed every sensual indulgence and paraded through the community like a prince, all in pure mimesis, following the pattern of satanic seduction Quetzalcoatl underwent by surrendering his power to the double in Tezcatlipoca's smoking mirror. Then, at the consummate moment of the sacramental mime, the victim was led to the temple altar where his heart was cut out and held up in offering to the blood-hungry Sun, ultimate image of devitalization, counter-magic to life itself.

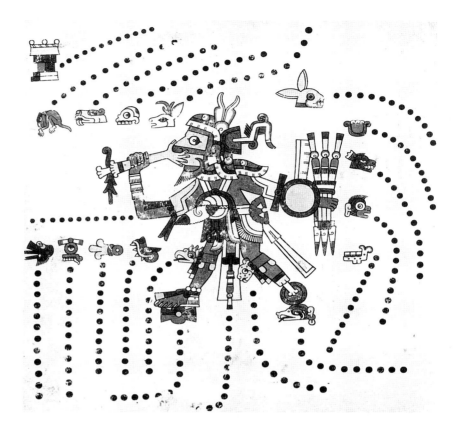

Tezcatlipoca, Lord of the Smoking Mirror, is the arch example of a black magician who uses mirror-power and double magic to achieve his end. Here the mirror he used to dupe Quetzalcoatl is shown (behind his left ear) as a dark semicircle, from which emanates the Aztec emblem for a plume of smoke ('smoking mirror'). (Aztec Codex. Tezcatlipoca.)

To be 'taken over' (motif of transference) or united with the double is fatal but, to complicate matters even more, total separation from it is equally fatal. Across diverse cultures and times, there is a universal consensus that the sighting of the double is a warning of imminent death. Although normally invisible, the double of each person becomes condensed, as it were, a few days before death. In peasant societies, especially, tales abound of glimpsing the double as it flees someone's hut at twilight, or slips into the woods beyond the village. In English folklore, the apparition of the doubles of those who will die in the course of a year can be seen at midnight of St Mark's Eve, but usually the exit of the double is quite haphazard and unpredictable. Sometimes it is seen by the person due to die, but more often by others.

Doubling is both a simple and an enormously intricate affair. In the mirror we are all doubled and few of us get the chance, like Alice, to find out what it's like on the other side. The *Malleus Maleficarium*, a dossier against witchcraft, states that those in league with the devil use mirrors to lure recruits, or even that the devil himself uses the mirror to spy on vain people. The vampire also occupies a curious niche in mirrorlore. As a member of the 'living dead', a vampire is the double of a once-living person, but now the original of the double has been totally eliminated: as when, upon losing an original document, we are left with the xerox copy. Since the double (completely separated from its original) can have no double, the vampire has no reflection. The vampire, it seems, is a twin-type who may be viewed as representing the ultimate fate of Narcissus. Complete merging with the double produces complete devitalization, and so the vampire lives in perpetual need of refuelling itself off its victims, who in turn are turned into bloodsucking doubles.

Since the double is not merely a mirror-image of its original, but a semi-autonomous entity endowed with the power both to resemble its original and to assume other forms, it must be closely associated, both in figure and function, with those supernatural feats of *shapeshifting* common to the worldwide arts of shamanism. In European lore, Merlin was a consummate shapeshifter who could even confer his metamorphic power upon others. In this manner, he facilitated the conception of King Arthur by Uther Pendragon, King of Britain. When Uther became enamoured of Igraine, wife of Gorlois, Duke of Cornwall, her husband immured her at Tintagel, away from Uther's lustful designs. But Merlin conferred upon Uther the power to assume the exact form of Gorlois, unite with Igraine and conceive Arthur.

Deliberate and complex manipulations of the double, usually for sinister purposes, characterize the practice of black magic and sorcery, along the lines

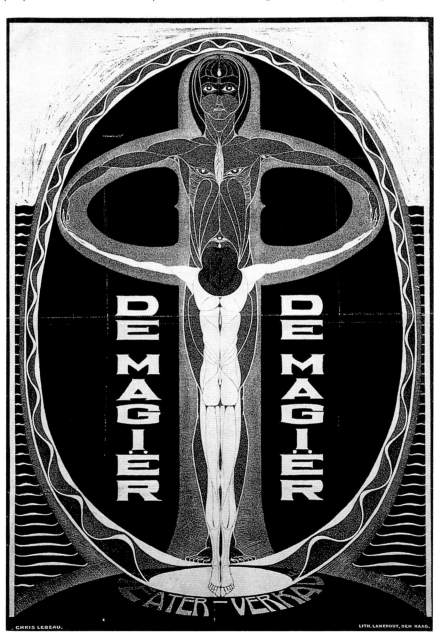

Fascination with the Double includes the satanic pretension that the dark 'other half' of the human soul is somehow more perfect and more powerful; therefore, subservience to it or union with it becomes desirable and may be sought through worship of the dark powers. (Poster: De Magier, the Wizard, by J.J. Christian Lebeau, c.1914.)

dramatically, and often hilariously, described by Carlos Castaneda. Bilocation figures strongly in these fantastic tales, for the double is said to co-exist simultaneously *and corporeally* with its original. It is even possible, in certain moments of shamanic befuddlement, to wander about not knowing if you are your double or – yourself, the one the double is based on. Feats of bilocation have been attributed to a number of Christian saints as well: Antony of Padua, Severus of Ravenna, Saint Clement and Saint Ambrose.

Far more common than these extravagant feats of doubling is the spontaneous experience of 'astral projection', or out-of-the-body experience, although here one does not always see the double which has become unaccountably liberated: one sees, instead, the inert original left behind. Tales of near-death experience also confirm the lore of the double. In Nepal and Tibet, the longstanding shamanic tradition of *Bon Po* includes the creation of *tulpas*, phantom-duplicates produced by epic feats of concentration. Madame Alexandra David-Neel, the first European to penetrate Tibet in the twentieth century, describes how, just for fun, she created such a double, a fat and jovial monk who accompanied her travelling party for several weeks and was alarmingly difficult to dissolve, apparently because he was having such a terrific time.

Fleetingly visible just before death, the double is spontaneously loosed in dreams as the 'dreaming body,' most likely identical to the vehicle of astral projection. Among the tribes around Lake Victoria, the double is called either *doshi* or *mzimu*, and it is believed to wander at large in the dream world. Peoples as far distant physically as the Eskimos and the Andaman Islanders agree that the double resembles its owner in form and figure to an uncanny degree (i.e., non-mirror-inverted). In the Dutch East Indies, the evil female double, called a nita, can impersonate a lover or friend. Those duped into sexual intercourse by these phantoms die in a few days. Among the Melanesians, the *atai* or 'mirror-soul' is just like the physical form but more fluid and powerful, capable of assuming all kinds of disguises such as the 'animal familiars' of European witchcraft. That black cat, by the way, is not the witch's pet, but the witch herself. The German word *doppelgänger* is the most common term for the double in Western anthropological studies.

Curiously, there appears to have been an outbreak of doublemania in Europe in the last half of the nineteenth century. Obsessions with the double occur widely in art and literature, especially in the milieu of Symbolist painting during the Decadence (centred around 1885) when occultism and satanic pretensions were all the rage. Dostoevsky wrote a famous novella about the double, and Gogol and other Russian writers treated it skilfully. Kafka's beetle is a metamorphic twin of the poor Gregor. While Bram Stoker and others were penning lurid tales of the Vampyre, Robert Louis Stevenson produced the classic tale of Dr Jekyll and his monstrous double, Mr Hyde. In America, Poe and Hawthorne dabbled with the double theme, and at the fin de siècle Oscar Wilde contributed his harrowing tale of Dorian Gray, a cruel, narcissistic aesthete who manages to transfer all his despicable moral defects to a portrait of himself, then dies gruesomely when he finally destroys it.

These, and many more, artistic renditions of the double theme captivated a wide audience at the very time that Spiritualism was on the rise in drawing rooms across England and the Continent. Participants were invited to witness, first-hand, the so-called ectoplasmic extrusions of the vital fluid of the medium, taking on the form and figure of those who had passed beyond. Much photographic evidence of these manifestations was obtained, and in one case the double was weighed by comparing the weights of a near-to-death person and his corpse: the result, about 2 to 2½ ounces. A more sensational time can hardly be imagined, for the ectoplasmic double produced by trance mediums was found to be both visible and touchable. It appeared by most reports to consist of a waxy, opaque substance, uncannily cold, capable of passing freely through physical objects and moving other objects at a distance. Experiments performed by Russian parapsychologists in this century have confirmed and extended many of these phenomena.

Perhaps even more fascinating than these accounts are the legitimate testimonies from people such as Goethe and Guy de Maupassant of direct encounters with their own doubles in the full waking state. Goethe relates a meeting while riding upon a horse to visit a woman friend. Coming the other way he saw his exact similar dressed (as he was not) in a suit of light gray mingled with gold threadwork. Eight years later, on horseback again on the same road, he found himself dressed in that very manner.

Maupassant, a French writer with a penchant for the supernatural, was sitting at his desk one afternoon in 1889 when he saw himself enter the room, sit down opposite him, bury his head in his hands and begin to dictate the very words of the story that Maupassant was then writing. When finished, the apparition stood up and vanished before his eyes.

Witnesses to their own double agree upon a number of striking traits: the double has a ruddy, feral, over-energized cast, it glares and casts insolent looks, or laughs with a chilling, derisive edge, and it disappears instantly if the witness shows just a little too much agitation at its presence.

Adam produces Eve 'from his side', an example of mythological cloning. To redeem humanity from the sin of the Original Pair, Christ must appear as a spiritually pure Double who produces as his holy bride, the Church – according to Catholic dogma, at least. (Bartolo di Fredi: The Creation of Eve.*)*

Goethe, Maupassant and others were able to witness their own double and, for some reason, not expire, but the English Romantic poet, Shelley, was not so lucky. Prone to hallucinations from childhood, Shelley first saw his double strangling his wife, Mary – she, the author of *Frankenstein*, another classic tale using the theme of monstrous projection. Not too long after this, while living in Italy in the summer of 1822, he encountered his double as he strolled on the veranda one evening. The apparition struck him, as if physically, with an impetuous, scorning look and demanded, 'How long do you mean to be content?' This was on June 24th, and by the 8th of July Shelley was dead, having drowned in a boating accident.

As a metamorphic twin, the double appears to embody the most powerful aspects of the strange conflictual bond that unites twins, making them firm but often unwilling partners in both life and death.

Scapegoat and Sacrifice

If identity can be substituted or even entirely displaced via metamorphic twinning, as we have just seen, then sacrifice, as the ultimate form of substitution, must also be the ultimate act of mythical transformation. As indeed it is, for sacrifice entails the 'ultimate sacrifice': death as the unique means for the transference of power from one being to another or one realm to another. The supreme case of twinning occurs in the scapegoat, the sacrificial double, the one who suffers or dies in the place of another. Again we encounter the radical ambivalence of the Sacred, here revealed in its most profound and paradoxical aspect. Twinning occurs in the most tragic sense when the scapegoat, chosen as the substitute for the original, must assume the suffering due to the original, even to the point of exile and death. Ritually, this choice is made as arbitrary as possible, using divination or lots and assuming total unconcern for the identity of the actual perpetrator.

Among the Dinka and the Ndembu, tribes of central Africa, the rite of sacrificial twinning still occurs in pure and ruthless form. To restrain the danger of blood-feuds leading to escalating cycles of aggression and retaliation, these people resort to a simple and elegant solution. They choose a sacrificial victim from the totemic clan or blood family of the offending party, *someone known to be innocent*, who then embodies a collective substitution, performed at the expense of the victim, for the purpose of maintaining peace in the community. Once the scapegoat is sacrificed, the offended parties are duly compensated and there is no more immediate threat of retaliatory violence within the community.

Here the scapegoat is clearly the twin of the victim (the person injured or murdered by the offending parties) as well as the instrument for the victim's retribution. And how could a more efficient solution be found, considering that in such societies there exist no legal and juridicial agencies capable of apprehending the perpetrator and holding a proper trial to see that justice is done? Among these African societies, when a crime is committed, all eyes are intent upon locating, not the perpetrator among the offending party, but a stand-in acceptable in the eyes of the offended party. Since there is no unbiased agency to apprehend, prosecute and punish the offender, no time is wasted looking for him or her. And so it has been in human societies in many parts of the world, down through the ages until our time.

The ideal scapegoat must itself be free of any traits of guilt. Radical substitution of this kind exemplifies the most profound level of twinning so far devised by the human species. The paramount case, of course, is Christ as the scapegoat of all mortal sin. Christ is the twin of humanity in more than one sense – indeed, in a series of replicating and inter-referring senses.

In the first place there is Adam, not so much the 'first man' but in the archetypal sense the ideal prototype of humankind – 'Adam Kadmon' of the Cabala. In the Genesis version, he twins himself and produces Eve, the clone-wife. Temptation by the Serpent (interpreted above) results in the 'fall' of the Pair and the necessity for a 'Second Adam' to come and redeem the sin of the first, which is now borne through the generations, rather like a genetic disorder, down to all of Adam/Eve's offspring, a long-term horizontal transference.

The next twinning after Adam/Eve occurs in the First Adam/Second Adam on a vertical axis, ontologically, and so requires an act of transcendent intervention to correct it. This is achieved through Christ who represents the Second Adam and so yields yet another twinning: Second Adam/Christ. Then, since Christ restores humanity to its total and uncorrupted potential before the Fall, the next implied twinning is none other than Christ/Humanity, the foundation of Christian theology. Christ is the image of ideal humanity, even of human divinity: in other words, the transcendent double of humankind. Through the sacrificial act of incarnation Christ is transformed into a unique hybrid, a one-and-only case of the ultimate twinning: divine/human, God/Man, Christ/Jesus.

Within the drama of Christ's mortal term, the profusion of twin-motifs continues. We find that John the Baptist, who announces the Lord's coming, has the same prenatal relation to Jesus as applies to twins who share one womb. Not long after the Annunciation, Mary goes to tell her glad tidings to Elizabeth, the woman who, in rather advanced age, is already pregnant with the child John the Baptist. 'No sooner had Elizabeth heard Mary's greeting, than the child leaped in her womb,' as we are told in Luke 1:41. The John-foetus, destined to proclaim the advent of the incarnated Word, quickens at the very first word announcing the presence of the Jesus-foetus.

As the twin-emissary of Christ, John both facilitates and impedes his coming, for although he calls together those who will become the audience receptive to Jesus, John must be eliminated before the ministry really begins. John himself expresses his awareness of this situation with gnomic precision: 'He must grow, I must disappear.' Apparently, the Christ/Baptist relation resembles a mathematical equation in which Jesus Christ and John the Baptist are quantities that 'vary inversely' to each other.

Twinning is rampant in the Christ Mythos, where mimesis and substitution, sacrifice, scapegoating and transference multiply in a dazzling display of motifs. As if all this were not enough, Christ is even credited with a biological twin brother, Thomas Didymus or Judas Thomas: in the Greek dialect of the New Testament, *didymos ton Christou*, literally, 'the twin of Christ.' Judas Thomas, ambivalently equated with the doubting Thomas, is said to resemble the Saviour in face and figure, in his actions and even in his redemptive powers. To him are attributed the 114 *logia* in the Gnostic *Gospel of Thomas*, and his life is fully described in the apocryphal *Acts of Thomas* found with other manuscripts at Nag Hammadi, Egypt, in 1945. These texts were used extensively by the Manichean theologians of radical dualistic persuasion to refute the monotheism of the early Church Fathers. One Gnostic heresy, Docetism, took the dualism to the point of claiming that it was not the human Christ but a phantom-double that underwent the Crucifixion.

The plaintive innocence of Xipe Totec, the Flayed God of the Aztecs, bears mute but eloquent witness to the role of the scapegoat who must be free of sin or blemish in order for its sacrifice to be effective. (Xipe Totec figure.)

As we have seen (in the second section), Persian theology of the most archaic era reflects a radical dyadic structure that may be considered the base-stratum of all subsequent versions of the saviour mythos. Indeed, the celestial, pre-cosmogonic conflict between Ohrmazd and Ahriman is beautifully repeated in the 'Hymn of the Pearl', a long passage in the *Acts of Thomas* that renders the Gnostic redeemer myth in concise and poetical language. This allegory concerns a twin-soul consisting, like Jesus Christ, of divine and human components. The pure immortal essence of the human soul is represented as a young and innocent child, the 'king's son' who goes forth to face the world. He is accompanied by two companions known in Persian angel lore as the *parwanqua*, 'twin-guides' – his spiritual bodyguards, as it were. The pilgrimage of the king's son in the human world mirrors the Advent of Christ and provides the model for the self-transcending quest of the twin-soul repeated, over and over again, in Christian teachings.

All this is pre-Christian Gnosticism, adapted to the Incarnation from the second century onward. In the third century, Mani appears and revives Persian dualism in the form of the Manichean heresy. Mani himself claims to be impregnated, as it were, with the astral double of Jesus, and he is called *at-taum*, a transposition of the Aramaic *toma*, 'twin.' He is not only a twin to Christ (Jesus/Mani), but also to the Holy Ghost (Mani/Paraclete), an elegant four-way twin-structure in which Mani attempted, though unsuccessfully, to expand and humanize the Christian trinity of Father, Son and Holy Ghost. Jung cites the quaternity as the root-structure of 'God' as archetype of the Self.

In fact, the dyadic structures informing the Saviour Mythos not only designate Jesus Christ as the ultimate mythic twin, but also involve us in working out what purports to be the resolution of the non-resolving Duad: perfect fusion of divine and human, immortal and mortal. The alchemists of the late Middle Ages were especially sensitive to this self-scapegoating miracle, which they saw as the supreme act of self-empowerment. For them the Risen Saviour (depicted emerging from a sarcophagus in some alchemical drawings) is not a superterrestrial phantom but something like a supra-biological germ-cell, capable of infinite replication of 'resurrection bodies': Christos is the seedpower for twinning to the nth degree.

Viewed anthropologically, the Crucifixion is a specific case of the rites of 'sacred kingship' widely discussed by Frazer in *The Golden Bough*. In theocratic systems the same rules apply as those found in totemic societies: the King or clan-head is a stand-in for the entire blood-clan – a 'group-soul vehicle,' in esoteric terms. Along with the power and privilege of the king, protected by many taboos, comes the responsibility of the sacrificial twin whose eventual death will insure both the vital and spiritual continuity of the group: motif of substitution. Therefore the king, especially in the time prior to his ritual sacrifice, is allowed to violate all taboos, to perform all the acts that would, if performed by anyone else, bring terrible ills and calamities upon the community, exactly as applies for the assigned twin of Quetzalcoatl in the Aztec rites.

In the widest sense, sacrifice appears in all cosmogonic myths where a supreme being becomes, through immolation, the foundation of the world-process. 'In the beginning was the Word,' which immolates itself in Christ to refound the world. In some cases the immolation is self-occasioned; in many others it results from the conflict between twin deities, twin brothers, but most often it comes about through a dramatic act of sacrificial twinning. The scapegoat is the first choice and last resort of all redemptive technologies, the most efficient exploitation of the dyadic nature of the Sacred.

Lovers and Soul-Mates

Viewing lovers as twins, we are again reminded of the primary operation of Desire in all cosmic pairings. In human love, the power of primary attraction (Desire), the draw toward harmony and interfusion, is what bonds the lovers against all influences to the contrary, all forces of discord and separation (Division) of the kind that may indeed arise from within themselves as well as from the outer world. In the tension between these two are woven a thousand plots. Love is the quest of the Twin to find itself through the Other.

As we have seen, twinning runs so deep into the realm of mythical construction that specific twin-motifs are most vividly revealed by examining the most archaic materials available. This proves truer than ever in the case of the twin/lover motif, illustrated in the Persian creation-myth drawn from the *Bundahish* and *Zatsparam* composed of late recensions of very early materials.

Here we find a creation-myth closely conflated with the scenario of the primeval pair, twin-lovers. Ohrmazd and Ahriman are the 'twin sons' of Zurvan, as we noted earlier, apropos the conflictual symbiosis of twin deities. The two brothers wrestle in the womb and after Ahriman breaks free, claiming the right of primogeniture, he becomes the Demiurge. This is a Gnostic term for a creator-god who is not first and original, alone and above it all, but merely the inferior or 'fallen' projection of the true Supreme Being. The Demiurge is the 'shadow' or metamorphic, inverted Double of the Creator. As such, Ahriman stands opposed to Ohrmazd who, as 'Primal Radiance', is a pure and faithful projection of the intention of the Creator.

Next, Ohrmazd creates Gayomart, the ideal prototype of humanity, but Ahriman attacks and kills it. Here the motif of competition is interplayed with the motifs of transference and sacrifice, for when Gayomart is destroyed, his constituent parts are scattered throughout the creation, still in its formative stages, where they become the 'seed-deposits' of the seven precious metals. As these metals correspond to the morphological patterning of the seven Sacred Planets, the immolation of Gayomart, while a victory of Ahriman, is also a victory of Ohrmazd. It insures the imprinting of the divine blueprint (Word, Logos) onto material creation: motif of replication on the cosmogonic scale.

Of the seven elements, part of the gold-seed grows into a plant from which emerges the first human couple. Typically, the First Parents are a perfect androgyne, intertwined as if in incestuous embrace and impossible to tell apart. As they mature, they assume the distinct form of the two sexes – exactly as occurs with twins in human biological reproduction. Here Mashya is male, the Persian Adam, and Mashyane is female, the Persian Eve. They eventually mate and give birth to twins in seven sets, perfect brother/sister pairs who in turn mate incestuously and produce the human race in all its variety. In the beginning was the Duad, and the Duad was incestuous, reproducing itself.

At some point the Evil One, called Angra Mainyu in later versions, causes the First Pair to quarrel and refrain from intercourse for fifty years. At the end of this period Mashya says, 'When I see your sex my desires rise,' and Mashyane replies, 'When I see your great desire rise, I too am agitated.' This is again a concise formula of Desire and Division, for the act of quarrelling and abstention (division) merely serves to intensify the moment of mutual attraction (desire), as when the sex is sweeter after the lovers have come through a fight or estrangement. The desire of the primordial pair is described in terms of libidinal mirroring, the lust of one reflecting the lust of the other.

In alchemy, the divine lovers appear at many stages of the Great Work, but their soul-bond is consummately strong in the 'incestuous water marriage,' when the primeval act of creation is re-enacted in a yogic rite of sacred coitus. The gesture of their crossing hands is an eloquent allusion to the ubiquitous 'handedness' of dyadic structure. (Alchemical water marriage, from John Dastin, De erroribus, *15th century.)*

From the dualistic theology of ancient Persia derives the Western problem of choice and the ethics of choice, a set of quandaries which, apparently, cannot be resolved unless the dynamics of intimate love provide a solution. Choosing and loving are twinned, even if love disguises itself, trickster-fashion, in the trappings of fickle and irresistible forces such as sexual chemistry. The quest for love as the resolution of free will begins for the West in Plato and moves like a momentous current through the troubadours in the late Middle Ages right up to its climax of nineteenth century Romanticism.

Scholars agree that the romantic psychology of the troubadours was deeply influenced by the survival of Persian dualism under Mani, the flayed heretic of Mesopotamia. He is said to have had a spirit-twin and protective genius, *suzugos*, a word containing the Indo-European root *zugos* or *yugos*, the same as the Sanskrit word yoga, the basis of 'yoke' in English. This term was exploited in the dualistic theology of Manicheanism to describe the consubstantiality of celestial and terrestrial, divine and human elements in the human being. This theological dyad then passes over into the theory of romantic love.

In this theory, alive and thriving to this day, the lost or 'fallen' component of the human soul is sought through its projection into the beloved. This is the basis of the troubadour aesthetic and related forms of Arabian mysticism in which the woman was idolized as a lens for attaining mystic vision of the spiritual essence of oneself: motif of twinning via substitution and transference, once again. The medieval troubadours adopted this mystical technique from Arabian sources, but then slipped into the typically Western fate of falling for the woman herself, rather than the mystic vision for which she was supposed to serve as a catalyst and grounding device.

Romantic love is the search for the divine essence in another, with the aim of twinning or mating it to one's own. It is also the greatest device for self-alienation on earth. The mystic quest for the love-twin threatens radical otheration for the seeker.

The psychology of lover-twins was set forth by Shelley in his short essay 'On Love.' Here the poet describes love as the 'powerful attraction' to what we imagine or believe must lie beyond ourselves 'when we find within our own thoughts the chasm of an insufficient void'. In other words, incompletion felt deep in the self seeks resolution through another. What Shelley means by our own thoughts is our entire capacity for reflection, including the thought of 'self'. Usually, this carries us quite well, reminds us that we are who we are, a certain entity with a certain identity. In mental self-reflection, we are all Narcissus, gazing endlessly at our own image, the 'I' in our thoughts. But there are moments, as everyone knows, when this 'I' fails us. It grows weak and seems, suddenly, to be lacking a foundation. We become doubtful of ourselves, lonely, empty and afraid. We confront an inner void.

Love, writes Shelley, 'thirsts after its likeness'. Is this the likeness of the inner void, or of that which is believed capable of filling it? In the extreme compression of the essay, this probably means that love is the power in us which thirsts after *the likeness of the inner 'I' in its complete and self-confirming status*. Through love, the 'I' is reconfirmed to itself *by something outside itself* – validation it sorely needs when it feels all inner resources to be exhausted.

This self-finding through the other is, moreover, necessary for the ultimate health of the soul. If it were adequate for the self to know itself through itself alone, it would succumb to Narcissistic absorption, ultimately rendering it incapable of loving anything or anyone beyond itself. Thus love, Shelley proposes, strives for its 'antitype', its twin and counter-image, preferably embodied in another person who reflects to us, as a mirror does, the ideal and complete essence within ourselves, the 'soul within the soul.' In addition to this wonderful mirroring, the twin-lovers resonate to all the measures of *both* our internal and external worlds. The romantic twin is a perfect fit.

Here is the formula for romantic infatuation, or Narcissism squared. In practice, it is a vale of sweet agonies and stunning contradictions. Shelley's passion for his wife Mary, the author of *Frankenstein*, is a vivid chronicle of how the theory plays out in real-life. In Jungian terms, this is classical anima-possession provoking a reciprocal case of animus-projection. Soul-twinning can be an endless lover's quarrel. On the other hand, lovers taken as twins often get along famously, and even may produce a brood of creative, not just biological, offspring.

The theory of soul-mates is obviously pure Platonism, its earliest version to be found in Aristophanes' account of the split-up androgyne, told at the beginning of the *Symposium*.

Shelley gives artistic expression to the theory in his long poem, 'Epipsychidion', inspired by meeting a 19-year-old Italian girl, Emilia Viviani, the 'Emily' of the poem. She is the externalized soul-woman, the spiritual twin of the poet. *Epipsyche* is Shelley's term for the miniature of our entire self, divested of all we detest about ourselves, the germ of pure and flawless self-love which may also be conceived as the seat of spiritual essence in the 'I'. It is the 'ideal prototype' of the Beautiful. The poet, the true seeker after Beauty, indraws all the beauties of the sensorial world to this point of internal focus, rather like an antenna-dish

Romantic love, based on the theory of twin-souls derived from Orphic philosophy via Plato, maintains that the sexual-erotic chemistry of bodies is a symptom of the magnetism between two souls seeking to unite (or re-unite) into a lost wholeness. With every kiss, the One passes over into the Other. (Fuseli: The Kiss.*)*

collecting signals from outer space, then projects it out again upon an external person. In short, unable to find the essence of self-love in himself, the poet draws the elements for it from the surrounding world and fixes it at an inaccessible (in fact, uncreated) point within his soul. To come into full possession of himself, he must somehow merge with it via the essence and figure of another.

Whether or not the soul-twin who bears this essence arouses Eros in the poet is a tricky question, for the law of desire-and-division undergoes considerable warpage in the heat of romantic experimentation. Shelley was tormented by the disparities between Platonic and Erotic love, which he could not resolve. Presumably, finding the lover-twin produces an impact in one's own soul which consolidates the spiritual essence of the 'I', something one is powerless to do on one's own. Shelley specifies that in the soul there is a chaos of emotional elements ('mine') quite distinct from the concentrated germ of the 'me'. The soul-mirroring woman fixates the *me*, first by her outer image, then by the impact of her love upon the emotional life of the lover.

> To the intense, the deep, the imperishable,
> Not *mine* but *me*, henceforth be thou united
> Even as a bride, delighting and delighted.

Lovely as it sounds, this interaction is fraught with conflict because the beloved, as well as being the soul-mirroring twin, is an independent self and fully other person; and the effect of otherness is stifling, disruptive, confrontational. Here, in essence, is the warring love-bond of Twins, enacted through romantic passion with all its mergings and cross-projections. Shelley could not tolerate the full impact of the other upon his soul, even though he longed for it with all his being. For him sexual contact was a disruptive 'electric fire.' The quest for the twin-soul was for him a way to ultimate self-perfection, not union with another.

When William Blake, another Romantic concerned with these issues, wrote in his *Proverbs in Hell* that 'The most sublime act is to set another before you,' he was using the word 'sublime' in the idiom of the day to mean something awesome and terrible, beyond human reckoning or control. Spiritual twinning is a Titanic love-affair, overwhelming the meagre strength of human needs. Shelley himself could not achieve it and over-idealized the process, finally losing to his private demons right down to the blood-chilling face-off with his Double.

Because the Duad is conflictual, and human nature itself is dyadic in structure, we must 'make love' of the Two, but how to do it so it stays made has never yet been revealed.

Genetics, Cloning and the Biological Duad

Considered genetically, the matter of Twins returns us to the realm of cosmic origins, literally to the cellular dimension, the genetic matrix of life itself. In the vast swirling sea of nucleic acids of which we are embodied, DNA is the informing dyadic structure, the 'double helix'. It is life and the intelligence of life, the master coding system that generates all organic and cognitive functions in human, animal and plant. Working with it is RNA, its twin acid and replicating medium, the agent of the innermost functions of twinning.

All life is replication. Of twinning are we born. This is both a scientific verity and one of the oldest theological propositions on the planet. In the *Gospel of*

John the opening line implies twinning by its paratactical structure: 'In the beginning was the Word and the Word was God and the Word was with God . . .' The Word, the power which produces all creation, is both the source of what it creates and the blueprint for creating it. As the Word which both IS and IS-WITH, the cosmogonic Logos is dynamically twinned *ab origine*. As the living breath informing and interfusing all things, God is the supreme morphological field – and the field is a Duad.

In the realm of living creatures, the vast complex of cells composing the body of a sexually reproducing entity derives in its totality from a single unit, the zygote, by a long series of successive divisions. The original cell first divides into two (mitosis), then these two into four, and so forth. With each division the amount of DNA doubles and complex structures such as mitochondria are created. The process is pure twinning, completely uniform from unicellular algae right up through plants and animals to *homo sapiens*.

To comprehend the enormous potency of the twin-dynamic at work here, consider the Persian legend of a wily beggar who gets the Shah to grant him one wish, although the Shah only agrees on the condition that the wish not be too extravagant. Pointing to a chessboard, the beggar says, 'Give me one grain on the first square, two on the second, four on the third, eight on the fourth, and so on until the board is full.' Pausing briefly to ponder this request, the Shah concludes it cannot amount to all that much. After all, he owns vast stores of grain, bases his wealth upon them, and can certainly afford to spare a little. Some weeks later when all the grain required to fill the board to the 64th square has been gathered, he finds himself as impoverished as the beggar – was.

In mitosis the chromosomal make-up of the original cell is repeated in the daughter cells, building massively into the mature organization of the body, but for the fully formed creature to *reproduce itself*, another kind of division must occur. This is meiosis, a reductive division in which the genetic material *halves itself*, rather than doubles. With this halving the constituent chromosomes are redistributed and the full number of 46 to a cell (called the haploid number) is split to 23 (diploid number). While mitosis (cell-doubling) occurs in all growing tissues, meiosis (cell-halving) only occurs in the sexual organs when nature is preparing gametes, or mating cells, for reproduction.

The human embryo is produced from an ovum in the mother's body that has been fertilized by a sperm from the father. Fertilization is, precisely speaking, the fusion of one gamete from each parent into a unique zygote, the single cell from which a whole, new, independent organism will evolve. The fusion of gametes, reproductive cells of 23 chromosomes each, determines all hereditary patterns. Genetics is the study of which combinations of 23 chromosomes occur and how they occur.

In normal, singleton births, one zygotic egg forms within the ovum, and begins developing even when the egg is sliding down the oviduct to find its lodgings in the womb. In twin births, two variations occur. With fraternal or non-identical twins, *two* eggs are involved all along the way, due to two distinct ova having been penetrated by two sperm at the time of fertilization. These twins have separate placentas and quite different genetic make-ups; they are not close look-alikes. With identical twins, involving one ovum and one sperm like a normal birth, the fertilized ovum *splits unnaturally* at some point in its development and two embryos, both sharing the same placenta, develop side by side with two identical sets of genes.

The formation of identical twins is deeply rooted in the mystery of biological creation itself. Reproduction *is* twinning, but only in rare instances does it offer

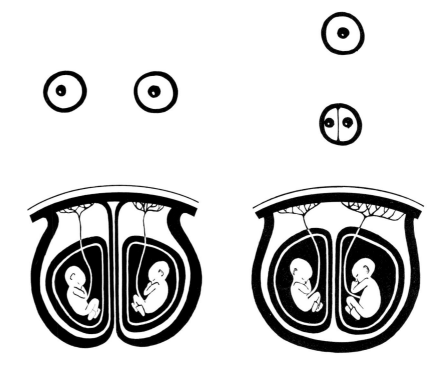

Twins may form in separate placentae (fraternal) or in a shared placenta (identical), each with their own umbilical cord. In some cases, however, the umbilical cords will become tangled, giving clear evidence for the mythological theme of twins battling in the womb.

us a literal representation, as it were, of its own internal activities. When it does, parity is demonstrated with astonishing precision. Mirror-symmetry is striking in identical, one-egg twins and, in Siamese twins, can be positively supernatural. Parity, let's recall from an earlier section, is exhibited everywhere in that feature of universal formation called 'handedness.' In all vertebrates, it shows up as *bilateral asymmetry*: meaning that the two halves of the body, right and left, are matched but not fully symmetrical. Compare the print-whorls of your thumbs for direct proof of this.

Siamese twins are so named because of the famous pair, Chang and Eng, born of Chinese parents in Siam in 1811. At the age of thirteen the boys were discovered by a British merchant, just as the King of Siam was about to have them put to death in the belief that they portended grave ill for his country. Eventually they were acquired by the circus magnate, P. T. Barnum, who exhibited them for years in his side-show of freaks. Chang and Eng were conjoined in a narrow area along their lower sides. They possessed complete sets of independent viscera but shared the same rectum.

Siamese twinning is due to a one-egg embryo splitting at a rather late phase, a 'late twinning division' as one theory maintains. If the division at any stage, early or late, is incomplete, conjoined bodies result. If the division is extremely early, the two children will be born physically separate, as identical twins who resemble one another as mirror-image duplicates. Both in Siamese twins and separate identical twins, the bodily organs and physical features (such as hair-whorls, handedness and fingerprints) are mirror-inverted: meaning that the features of one look like that of the other as they would appear in a mirror.

Behaviourally, most twins (apart from the Siamese sets who must, by necessity, lead extraordinary lives) are quite normal people, content to pursue their lives like everyone else. What does distinguish them is often an uncanny sense of symbiosis, the feeling of living simultaneously with or through the body, mind and emotions of the other. Twins are highly empathic with each other and may even be distinctly telepathic, knowing what is happening in each other's lives without needing the usual means of communication. They can be deeply dependent upon each other, emotionally and psychologically, and it is very common, when one twin dies, for the other to feel imbalanced and disoriented in a profound way. Perhaps twinhood is as close as nature dares to place us to the romantic dream of twin-souls interfused by the power of love.

For human twins to be so close, psychologically, that they simulate some of the patterns of mythological twins, their relationship must have become pathological. In the well-observed case of the so-called silent twins, June and Jennifer Gibbons, born in England in 1963, the pathology evolved to fantastic extremes. Unwilling to speak or react to the outside world, they developed their own secret language at about the age of four. Into their teens they lived as virtual recluses, writing profusely, making dolls and scripting elaborate histories for them, putting on their own radio shows for each other, utterly self-contained and hostile to intrusions. Physically, they imitated each others gestures with a weird mechanical precision. At eighteen they emerged into social life, trading a pair of binoculars back and forth as they looked for boys around town. They rapidly took up drugs, stealing and arson, developing into full-scale psychopaths, yet all the while exhibiting the most amazing feats of intellectual ingenuity, writing and publishing novels, taking courses in witchcraft, keeping endless journals. Upon being imprisoned they grew even closer but fell periodically into murderous fights, or suffered near-death depressions when separated. A pattern emerged in which the younger twin, Jennifer, seemed to assume the role of the evil one who dominates the other, reverting back to archaic symbiotic conflict – a pattern, however, broken for ever when one twin recently died.

Temperamentally, twins often exhibit close similarities and drastic contrasts but no *consistent* pattern of common behaviour and attitude. They may be 'psychically attuned', sharing moods like a pair of chameleons taking on each other's colours, but never, or rarely, in such a rigorous and uncanny fashion as the Gibbons twins. Healthy twins are, after all, independent entities, except for those cases of Siamese sets where the conjoining is very close (two heads on one body, or two sets of legs on a body with one head). Even so, Chang and Eng, the namesake duo, were in fact so independent that one, Chang, was quite a drinker, while the other, Eng, did not drink at all. Since they did not share any of the same internal organs, this was not a problem. More closely joined twins, such as the Bohemian sisters, Rosa and Josepha Blazek, may still exhibit a great degree of autonomy. One could be sick while the other remained well. Josepha, shorter and heavier of the two, had incomplete sexual organs in the pelvic area where they were joined, but Rosa was quite normal and even bore her own child. These twins were very active physically, climbing trees when young, learning several languages together and both playing the violin.

Statistically, Siamese twins occur in about one out of 100,000 births. Fraternal twins occur at about one in 86 births, with a high incidence in Belgium, Finland and the region of Africa inhabited by the Yoruba, one of the tribes to whom the twin is an omen of good fortune.

Nature produces twins, seemingly, at her own whim, but with recent advances in genetics it may become possible some day for every one of us to twin ourselves. Just 20 years after Watson and Crick worked out the dyadic structure of DNA in 1953, further experiments already led to the first success with recombinant DNA: the method of cutting and splicing the DNA strand, roughly in the way a plant is cut and grafted. This practice with plants is the prototype of

The Chulkhurst sisters, Siamese twins from Biddenden, in Kent, can be traced only as far back as 1645, but according to local tradition they were born in 1100 and lived to the age of 34. The way they are joined illustrates the close mirror symmetry that results from the late twinning division of a single egg after right-left anatomical differences have been well developed.

The modern science of cloning has its mythological prototype in the Flood legend which describes Noah gathering all the animals in pairs into his ark. Today's counterpart to the ark is clearly the test tube or Petri dish. (Venetian mosaic, San Marco.)

'cloning', the exact duplication of an organism by manipulation of its DNA. Cloning can produce an unlimited number of twins – theoretically, at least.

The awesome twin genius of human evolution appears to be the 'GENOME', an entity as mysterious as Adam Kadmon, the First Man of the Kabala. Every individual inherits from its parents a set of 'codes' for constructing and operating all the proteins in the body. The word 'gene' is applied to the code-sequence for each protein. The genome, then, is the total complement of genes in any individual make-up; hence, the master code-sequence of organic individuality.

In 1986, James Watson inaugurated the Human Genome Project with the aim of mapping an entire sequence consisting of an estimated three billion base pairs. Of these only about five percent, mysteriously enough, seem to be actual genes. The function of the remaining ninety-five percent is still unclear. Although the project is far from complete, some results of the work already done have found direct applications: for instance, genetic finger-printing, which has now been successfully applied to solving murder and rape cases.

DNA, the double helix, is perhaps the ultimate Twin of our modern mythology. Twinhood is the generative cipher of all desire and division. If Twins have been awesome to our ancestors since time immemorial, they are no less so today, though in a different manner, for the 'primitive mentality,' far from being over and gone, comprises the deep-set ontological structure of mind as we know it. Where our forebears resorted to sympathetic magic, secret naming, totemic replications, masks, mime, dances, symbols and animations painted on cave walls for supernatural attunement to twins and twinning, we turn to genetics. If science can indeed put us in touch with the deepest sources of life, it will have achieved its highest mission. Whatever the outcome, Twins will be there at the end as they were at the beginning.

In Greco-Latin mythology the most famous instance of twin births (twice over!) is certainly the nativity of Castor and Pollux, Helen and Clytemnestra. Born simultaneously from two eggs, they illustrate by strict biological definition the two cases of identical and non-identical twins (after Leonardo da Vinci, *Leda and the Swan*).

Myth rarely preserves such literal features, however, and so we never hear that Clytemnestra, tempestuous avenger of the House of Atreus, is identical in face and figure to Helen, reputed to be the most beautiful of all women. Their adversarial role as twins is utterly clear, nonetheless: Clytemnestra must counteract the evils caused by the beauty of Helen. They share the torments of mortal desire and blood-feud in the same way as Castor and Pollux share the mystery of immortality. Leda, the mother of both pairs, was visited by Zeus in the form of a swan, a metamorphic double of the kind that often appears in shamanic lore.